Senses

KINGFISHER
LONDON & NEW YORK

First published in as *Kingfisher Young Knowledge: Senses* in 2004
Additional material produced for Kingfisher by Discovery Books Ltd.

Distributed in the U.S. by Macmillan, 175 Fifth Ave., New York, NY 10010
Distributed in Canada by H.B. Fenn and Company Ltd.,
34 Nixon Road, Bolton, Ontario L7E 1W2

Library of Congress Cataloging-in-Publication data has been applied for.

ISBN: 978-0-7534-6452-6

Kingfisher books are available for special promotions and premiums.
For details contact: Special Markets Department, Macmillan,
175 Fifth Avenue, New York, NY 10010.

For more information, please visit www.kingfisherbooks.com

Printed in China
10 9 8 7 6 5 4 3 2 1
1TR/0410/WKT/UNTD/140MA/C

Note to readers: the website addresses listed in this book are correct at
the time of going to print. However, due to the ever-changing nature
of the Internet, website addresses and content can change. Websites
can contain links that are unsuitable for children. The publisher cannot
be held responsible for changes in website addresses or content or
for information obtained through a third party. We strongly advise
that Internet searches be supervised by an adult.

Acknowledgments
The publishers would like to thank the following for permission to reproduce their material. Every care has been taken
to trace copyright holders. However, if there have been unintentional omissions or failure to trace copyright holders,
we apologize and will, if informed, endeavor to make corrections in any future edition.
b = bottom, *c* = center, *l* = left, *t* = top, *r* = right

Cover main Shutterstock/Rick Becker-Leckrone; cover *l* Shutterstock/Renata Osinka; cover *r* Shutterstock/Andriy Petrenko; 1 Corbis; 2–3 Michael K. Nichols/National
Geographic; 4–5 Raymond Gehman/National Geographic; 6–7 Alamy Images; 9*r* Digital Vision; 10*cl* Adam Hart-Davis/Science Photo Library; 10–11*b* Sean
Murphy/Getty Images; 12*l* Piers Cavendish/ardea.com; 12–13*t* DiMaggio/Kalish/Corbis; 13*br* Jeff Lepore/Science Photo Library; 14*bl* NHPA/James Carmichael Jr.;
14–15*tc* NHPA/Stephen Dalton; 15*br* NHPA/Nigel J. Dennis; 17*br* Susumu Nishinaga/Science Photo Library; 18*l* Mark Baker/Reuters; 18–19*b* Roy Morsch/Corbis;
19*tr* Tony Marshall/EMPICS Sports Photo Agency; 20*l* NHPA/William Paton; 20–21*c* NHPA/Daryl Balfour; 21*br* Duncan McEwan/Nature Picture Library; 22*bl(l)* Joel
W. Rogers/Corbis; 22*bl(r)* Nick Gordon/ardea.com; 22–23*t* NHPA/ANT Photo Library; 23*br* Georgettte Douwma/Getty Images; 24*bl* NHPA/Stephen Dalton;
25*tr* NHPA/ANT Photo Library; 25*br* Dietmar Nill/Nature Picture Library; 26*l* Craig Hammel/Corbis; 27*tr* BSIP VEM/Science Photo Library; 27*br* Suzanne & Nick
Geary/Getty Images; 28*tl* François Gohier/ardea.com; 28–29*b* NHPA/Guy Edwardes; 29*tr* NHPA/Ann & Steve Toon; 30–31*b* Pascal Goetgheluck/ardea.com;
31*tr* John Downer Productions/Nature Picture Library; 31*br* Roy Morsch/Corbis; 32*br* Corbis; 33*b* Omikron/Science Photo Library; 34*l* NHPA/Martin Harvey; 34–35*b*
NHPA/T. Kitchin & V. Hurst; 35*tr* Matthew Oldfield, Scubazoo/Science Photo Library; 37*tl* Phil Jude/Science Photo Library; 38*l* Angelo Cavalli/Getty Images and Ryan
Mcvay/Getty Images; 38–39*b* NHPA/Kevin Schafer; 39*tr* Dr. Jeremy Burgess/Science Photo Library; 48*c* Shutterstock Images/ultimathule; 48*b* Shutterstock
Images/Vasiliy Koval; 49*t* Shutterstock Images/Kruglov_Orda; 49*b* Shutterstock Images/Andrew Armyagov; 52*c* Shutterstock Images/orionmystery@flickr;
52*b* Shutterstock Images/Eric Isselée; 53*t* Shutterstock Images/Annamaria Szilagyi; 53*b* Shutterstock Images/EcoPrint; 56*t* Shutterstock Images/Eric Isselée

Commissioned photography on pages 33, 36, and 42–47 by Andy Crawford
Thank you to models Corey Addai, Anastasia Mitchell, Sonnie Nash, and Shannon Porter

discover science

Senses

Jinny Johnson

KINGFISHER
NEW YORK

Contents

What are senses?

Imagine the world if you could not see things or hear your friends talking or if you could not smell and taste your food. We do not often think about our senses, but they tell us what is going on around us. We have five main senses. They are sight, hearing, smell, taste, and touch.

Super senses

Animals have senses, too. Some animals have better senses than we do. Dogs can hear sounds that humans cannot, and they have a much stronger sense of smell.

Using senses

This boy can see his pet's big brown eyes, feel his soft fur, and hear his grunting noises. He can also smell the roses in the background and can probably smell his dog.

The sense center

brain

Your brain controls your senses. Messages travel from your eyes, ears, nose, tongue, and skin to tell it what is going on. The messages travel along special pathways in the body called nerves.

Messages to the brain

Nerves go from the brain to all parts of your body. A message can zoom along the nerves to the brain in a tiny fraction of a second.

nerves

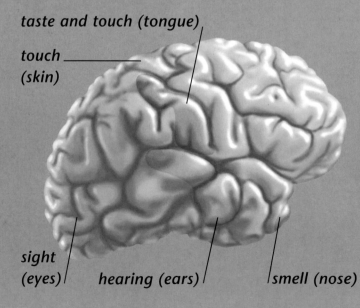

taste and touch (tongue)

touch (skin)

sight (eyes)

hearing (ears)

smell (nose)

Jobs for the brain

The brain sorts out the messages it receives from the nerves. Look at the picture on the left to see which parts of the brain sort out messages related to your senses.

brain

Keeping your brain safe

Your brain is inside your head. Feel your bony skull at the top of your head. It protects your brain. Your brain is usually fully grown by the time you are around six years old.

How do I see?

Your eyes make pictures of the outside world—similar to what a camera does. You can see big things and small things, and you can see many different colors.

pupil (black)

iris (brown)

Letting in light

The black circle in the middle of your eye is called the pupil. This is an opening through which light passes into your eye.

Eye color

The colored part of the eye is called the iris. It can be blue, green, or brown. What color irises do these children have?

Making a picture

When you look at something, light bounces off it and goes into your eye. Inside the eye the lens makes an image on the area called the retina, at the back of the eye. Messages about this image travel along nerves to the brain.

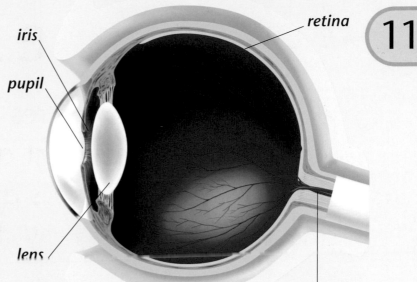

iris

pupil

lens

retina

nerves

bone in eye socket

Amazing eyesight

Some animals have excellent eyesight. Their eyes need to be right for the jobs they have to do— such as spotting food or looking out for danger.

Night eyes

Hunting animals, such as this cat, have powerful, forward-facing eyes that help them see details well and judge exactly where something is. Cats can see much better at night than we can.

Sharp sight

Birds of prey, such as this peregrine falcon, can see things from a long distance away. Its large alert eyes can spy a tiny mouse from high up in the air.

All-around view

Side-facing eyes help this mouse see as much of what is going on around it as possible. This means that it can spot any enemies—and has a chance to escape!

Different eyes

Not all animals have eyes like ours. Some animals have eyes that look very different but are perfect for helping them find food.

Spider eyes

Most spiders have eight eyes. But only the two large eyes in the front are used for seeing. The smaller ones sense movement and help the main eyes find prey.

Two directions

A chameleon stays very still as it watches for insects to catch. Its big, bulgy eyes can swivel around and even point in two directions at once.

Mini eyes

A dragonfly's eye is made up of 30,000 parts. Each one is like a tiny eye. They allow the dragonfly to see many images at high speed so it can track fast-moving prey.

chameleon

How do I hear?

Your ears allow you to hear sounds, from a quiet whisper to the loudest rock music. The outside parts of your ears pick up sounds and funnel them down inside your ears.

sound waves

Moving sounds
When something makes a noise, it creates movements in the air called sound waves. These travel into the ears, where hearing really happens.

fluid-filled tubes

tiny bones

nerve

eardrum

ear canal

cochlea

outer ear

Into the ear

Inside each ear there are an eardrum and a series of tiny bones. These vibrate when sound waves go into the ear. The vibrations travel straight into the ear.

Tiny hairs

Deep inside the ear, in the cochlea, are more than 15,000 tiny hairs. When sound vibrations reach these hairs, they move and send nerve messages to the brain—and you can hear.

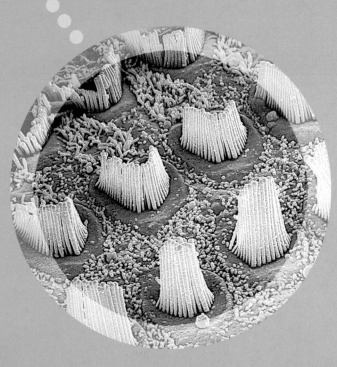

Staying balanced

As well as allowing you to hear sounds, your ears help you keep your balance. As you move around, tiny hairs inside fluid-filled tubes in your ears tell you which way up you are.

Seasickness

You may feel sick on a boat because your brain gets confused. Your ears tell it you are moving, but your eyes say you are not.

Dizzy spells

If you spin around and then suddenly stop, your ears do not get the message to your brain right away. Then you feel dizzy.

Practice makes perfect

Gymnasts do not get dizzy because they practice their moves over and over again so that their brains get used to the signals.

Animal ears

Ears come in all shapes and sizes. The ears of the African elephant are the biggest of all. They can be 6 feet (2 meters) long.

Listening for danger

A rabbit's long ears help it catch the tiniest sound that might mean danger is near. It can also swivel its ears to pick up sounds from different directions.

Faraway calls

Elephants can hear much deeper sounds than we can. They can hear the low calls of other elephants from several miles away.

Insect ears

Some insects have ears in surprising places. Crickets have ears on their front legs. This grasshopper has ears on each side of its body.

Listening underwater

The ocean may look like a silent world, but it is not. Sounds travel farther through water than air, and fish, whales, and other sea creatures can hear sounds.

Closed ears

An otter does not use its ears underwater. When it dives, it closes its ears so it will not get water in them.

Whale calls

The only parts of a whale's ears that you can see are the tiny holes on each side of its head. But whales have excellent hearing. A humpback whale can hear the calls of other whales from many miles away.

humpback whale

Listening fish

Fish have ears inside their bodies that allow them to hear what is going on around them. They make noises to stay in touch with one another and to listen for sounds of enemies—or food!

Sound pictures

Bats, whales, and dolphins are some of the creatures that have a special sense called echolocation. This means that they use sound instead of sight to make a "picture" of their surroundings.

Night hunters

Bats hunt at night and can catch an insect in complete darkness by using echolocation. As it flies, a bat makes many very high sounds.

"Seeing" sounds

Echolocation works in water, too. Dolphins find food in the deep, dark ocean by making sounds that echo and help them "see" their prey.

Sound echoes

When the bat's sounds meet an insect, they make echoes that bounce back to the bat's ears. The echoes tell the bat where its prey is, how big it is, and even how fast it is moving.

Smelling things

Your sense of smell happens inside your nose. The outer parts of your nose mostly warm and clean the air you breathe in before it travels to your lungs.

Achoo!

You sneeze when something irritates the inside of your nose and your body tries to force it out. The tiny hairs in your nose trap dust and dirt and stop them from getting into your lungs.

How you smell

When you smell something, tiny pieces of its scent travel into your nose. They go right to the top into two special sense areas. Nerves send messages from there to your brain, telling it about the smell.

A world of smells

For some creatures, the sense of smell is more important than sight. Many animals smell their enemies before they see them. Predators often hunt by smell.

Super nose

Bears have a very sharp sense of smell to help them find food. A polar bear can smell its prey from 12 miles (20 kilometers) away.

Life in the dark

Moles live underground, where it is so dark that eyes are not very useful. A mole finds its way around by using its senses of smell and touch.

Smell check

Every once in a while, deer take a break from feeding on grass and look up to sniff the air for any signs of danger.

Smelly messages

Many animals use smell to send messages to one another. These messages might say, "Stay away" or "I am looking for a mate." When a dog sniffs a tree, it can tell which other dogs have marked the same spot.

Special signals

When a female moth is ready to mate, she gives off a special scent. The feathery antennae on a male moth's head can pick up the smell from 3 miles (5 kilometers) away.

Smelly warning

A skunk uses smell to protect itself. If an enemy comes too close, the skunk squirts out a very smelly liquid from an area close to its tail.

My mark

When a cat rubs its cheeks against something, it is leaving a scent message. It is saying, "I was here. This is my patch."

Tasting things

Your sense of taste works with your sense of smell to tell you about the food you eat. You taste with your tongue. Taste helps you enjoy food, but it also warns you if something is not safe to eat.

Four flavors

There are four main flavors: bitter, salty, sour, and sweet. Most foods are a mixture of more than one of these. Different areas of the tongue are sensitive to certain flavors. Match the colors below to the picture opposite to see where these areas are located.

bitter   *salty*

sour   *sweet*

Taste buds

Your tongue is covered with about 10,000 tiny taste buds, which are too small to see. Each taste bud is sensitive to a particular kind of taste.

Bumpy tongue

Your taste buds are clustered around the little bumps you can see on your tongue. Nerves inside the taste buds send messages to your brain about what you are tasting.

Animal tastes

Like us, animals have taste buds on their tongues, but it is hard to know what they taste. Most animals probably use smell and taste to tell what is good to eat.

Good taste

Tigers—and pet cats—have sensitive tongues. They can taste different flavors in plain water.

Swimming tongues

Catfish are like swimming tongues—they have taste buds on their bodies that help them find food in the water. They can also taste food using their whiskers, which are called barbels.

Tasting toes

Butterflies taste with their feet and with their mouths. By using their feet, they know what kind of food they have landed on before they unroll their tongues to eat.

Touch and feel

You can feel with any part of your body because your skin contains many tiny nerve endings. These send messages to the brain about what you are touching.

soft

What does it feel like?

When you hold something, notice how it feels. It may be rough or smooth, sharp or soft, hot or cold. Our sense of touch tells us these things. It also lets us feel pain.

cold

sharp

smooth

hot

Sensitive skin

Some parts of your skin
can feel things better
than other parts. Fingers,
toes, and lips are very
sensitive. Most of your skin
is covered with tiny hairs.
These stand on end when
you are cold or scared.

Animal touch

Animals feel things with their skin, too. But some have extra ways of touching. Many animals have very sensitive whiskers that help them learn about their surroundings.

Super trunk
The tip of an elephant's trunk is the most sensitive part of its body. An elephant does many things with its trunk, from cuddling its young to picking up tiny leaves.

Hairy legs

A spider waits on its web for its prey. Hairs on the spider's legs sense the tiniest movement that might mean food is near.

Wet paws

A raccoon has very sensitive paws and whiskers. They are even more sensitive when they are wet, which may be why a raccoon wets its paws before eating.

Which line is longer?
Seeing involves your brain as well as your eyes. Sometimes your brain can be tricked into seeing something that is not really there.

You will need:
- Paper
- Colored pen or pencil
- Ruler

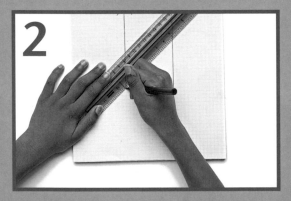

Using a ruler, draw a straight line that is 4 in. (10cm) long. Draw another 4-in. line beside the first line, about 2 in. (5cm) away.

On the first line, draw arrowheads pointing outward. On the second line, draw arrowheads pointing inward, as shown in step 3.

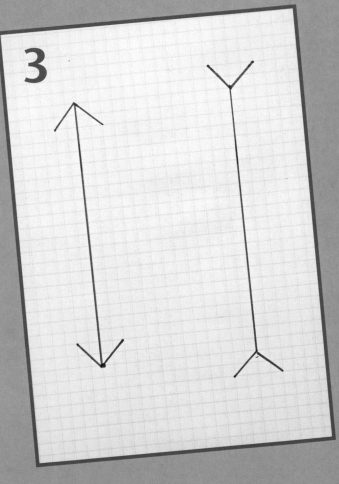

Look at the straight lines. Does one look longer than the other? The directions of the arrowheads trick your brain into thinking that one line is longer than the other.

Hole in the hand

Trick your eyes

Your brain can get confused if your two eyes see two different images. The brain puts the images together, and this can create a strange picture, like this illusion where you seem to see a hole in your hand.

1 Hold a cardboard tube up to your right eye. Then hold up your left hand next to the tube, with your palm facing you.

2 Look straight ahead. Your right eye should be looking through the tube and your left eye at your palm. Can you see a hole in your hand? Your eyes are playing tricks on your brain.

Model eardrum

How hearing works
Make a loud noise and you will see the stretched balloon on your model eardrum vibrate— just like your real eardrum does.

You will need:
- Balloon
- Scissors
- Plastic cup
- Rubber band
- Rice grains

Use scissors to cut off the neck of a balloon. Then carefully cut down one side so that you can open the balloon out flat.

Cut the opened-out balloon in half so you have a piece big enough to fit over the top of your plastic cup. This will be the eardrum itself.

Stretch the balloon over the cup. Attach it using the rubber band, keeping the balloon stretched as tightly as possible.

Sprinkle some rice grains on top of the balloon. Clap your hands or shout. Watch the grains jump as the stretched balloon vibrates.

Listening game

What can you hear?
Find a quiet spot and play this game—you will be surprised at the number of different sounds you hear.

You will need:
- Notebook
- Pen

Sit down with your notebook and pen. Listen carefully for sounds—a loud truck, birds singing, or a dog barking. Write down or draw pictures of the things you hear.

Guess the smell
You will be surprised at how difficult it is to tell what things are without looking at them, using only your sense of smell.

You will need:
- Scarf
- 5 plastic cups
- 5 smelly things: we used a banana, vinegar, a muffin, chocolate, and toothpaste

Ask a friend to sit down and let you tie a scarf over his eyes. Make sure it is tight enough that he cannot see, but not so tight that it hurts.

Add one smelly thing to each plastic cup. Then hold the first cup under your friend's nose and ask him to take a good sniff.

Ask him to guess what is in the cup just by smelling it.

Give your friend the other foods to smell one by one. See how many he can guess correctly. Some smells are hard to guess!

Guess the taste

Try guessing different drinks by taste alone. It can be difficult when you cannot see them, especially if some are similar.

You will need:
- Scarf
- 5 plastic cups
- 5 drinks: we used milk, chocolate milk, orange juice, apple juice, and water

1

Just like the smelling game, ask a friend to sit down let you and tie a scarf over her eyes. Make sure she is comfortable but cannot see.

Pour five different drinks into the plastic cups. Make sure you ask an adult which drinks you are allowed to use.

3

Ask your friend to take a sip of the first drink and guess what it is. Ask her to try each one and see how many she gets right.

Make a touch cube

Test your touch

This is a fun way to test your sense of touch. When you have made the cube, you can play with it or play a touch guessing game.

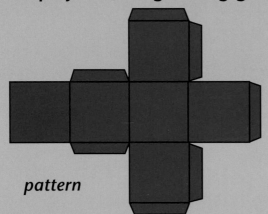

pattern

To make your touch cube, you will need to cut out a piece of cardboard in the pattern shown above. You might need to ask an adult to help you copy it.

You will need:
- Cardboard
- Pen
- Scissors
- Paper square
- Ruler
- Glue
- 6 different textured items: we used velvet, corrugated cardboard, cereal, a cotton pad, aluminum foil, and sandpaper

Place your paper square on the cardboard. Trace around it six times to make the pattern. Add flaps where shown in the pattern.

Carefully cut around the outside of the pattern, keeping all the edges as straight as you can. Then fold along all the lines.

3 Hold the middle square down with your finger and fold up the sides to make a box shape. Glue down the flaps to stick the box together.

4 Take some cereal shapes and carefully glue them to one side of the box to make a rough texture. You can use any kind you want.

5 Glue a different textured item to each of the other sides to make your cube. Ask a friend to close his or her eyes and guess the different items just by touching them.

48 Glossary

alert—if you are alert, you are paying attention to what is going on around you

antenna—a feeler on an insect's head (plural: antennae)

balance—the ability to stay upright and not fall over

brain—the structure inside your head that controls your body and allows you to think and have feelings

camera—a machine used for taking photographs

clustered—to be in a crowd, close together

confused—if you are confused, you don't understand something

echo—a sound that bounces off an object

enemy—something that wants to harm or eat you

escape—to break free from a place where you have been kept by force

eyesight—the ability to see

flavor—taste

fraction—a small amount

funnel—to direct something through a narrow space

gymnast—someone who is trained and skilled in gymnastics

image—a picture

irritate—if something irritates you, it causes you discomfort

lens—the part of the eye that focuses light

lungs—two large, spongy sacs in your chest that are used for breathing

nerves—special structures (like wires) that run from the brain to all parts of the body

ordinary—normal

predator—an animal that hunts and eats other animals

prey—an animal that is killed or eaten by another animal

scent—a smell

sensitive—able to feel or taste

signal—an action, sound, or gesture used to give a message to someone

skull—the bony part of your head that protects your brain

surroundings—the area and environment around you

swivel—to turn around in one spot

vibrate—to move rapidly back and forth

whiskers—long hairs on an animal's face

The content of this book will be useful in teaching, reinforcing, and enhancing many components of the science and language arts curricula. It can readily be applied to other areas of study across the curriculum.

Extension activities

Language arts
Writing
1) Imagine waking up with all your senses mixed up! What if you tasted with your feet, smelled with your ears, and heard with your fingers? Write a story about your day of mixed-up senses.

2) Make a list of adjectives that describe how different things feel (e.g. fuzzy, slimy, rough, hot). Give examples of things (nouns) that feel that way (e.g. fuzzy: peach, carpet, teddy bear).

Speaking and listening
Drop a small object such as a shell or plastic figure into a sock. Ask a friend to do the same and then exchange socks. Using only your sense of touch, reach in and find out everything you can about the object. Describe it out loud to your partner without calling it by name.

Science
Observation—using the five senses—is essential to scientific inquiry. The study of senses also relates to scientific themes of adaptations, structure and function, and diversity. Some specific links to science curriculum content include characteristics of animals (pp. 6–7, 12–15, 20–25, 28–29, 34–35, 38–39); the human body (pp. 6–11, 16–19, 26–27, 32–33, 36–37); behavior (pp. 12–15, 20–25, 28–31, 34–35, 38–39); and communication (pp. 6–7, 16–17, 20–25, 30–31).

Crosscurricular links
1) Geography, social studies, writing, and art: Choose a place you have been or would like to visit. Locate it on a map. Design a travel brochure describing what you might see, smell, hear, taste, and touch there.

2) Art: Use watercolor or tempera paint. Experiment with mixing red, blue, and yellow to create different shades and hues. Alternative media: use food coloring to dye white frosting. Mix colors to create new shades and then spread on a cracker for a snack!

3) *Art:* Look through the book for pictures of animal ears. Make several different types out of construction paper to fit around your own ears. What effect does each type have on your hearing?

Using the projects
Children can do these projects at home. Here are some ideas for extending them:

Page 40: Search the Internet for "optical illusions for kids." Print your favorites and start a collection. Make sure there is an adult with you.

Page 41: Point your index fingers together, not quite touching, a few inches in front of your eyes. Look past them to focus on the opposite wall. Do you see a floating "sausage?" Move your fingers apart and together to change the length of the "sausage." Your eyes are playing tricks on your brain again!

Pages 42–43: Play the "listening game" in the same location but at different times of the day and night. How do your lists of sounds compare?

Pages 44–45: Using the same procedure, take these activities a step further. Still using a blindfold, have the taster hold his or her nose while tasting each of the five liquids. How does the sense of smell influence the sense of taste?

Pages 46–47: Make a second cube with textures that are similar to each other, such as felt, velvet, and fur, or different cereal shapes. With practice, does it get easier to tell them apart?

Did you know?

- Most adult humans can tell the difference between about 10,000 different smells.

- Of all mammals, the giant anteater has the longest tongue in relation to its body size.

- Camels have three eyelids. The first two have very long lashes to stop sand from getting into their eyes. Their third eyelid is clear so they can see during a sandstorm.

- Worker bees have 5,500 lenses in each eye.

- Dogs have one million smell cells per nostril. Their smell cells are 100 times larger than a human's.

- A buzzard can see small rodents from a height of 14,800 feet (4,500 meters).

- Bluebottles taste with 3,000 sensory hairs on their feet.

- Earthworms have taste buds all over their bodies. They use them to sense their surroundings.

- Some people cannot tell the difference between red colors and green colors. They are said to be colorblind.

- Fingertips are full of nerve endings. People who are blind can use their sense of touch to read Braille, a kind of writing that uses a series of raised dots to represent different letters of the alphabet.

- A box jellyfish has 24 eyes!

- A newborn baby sees the world upside down because it takes some time for the baby's brain to learn to turn the picture the correct way up.

- Many crabs' eyes are located on the end of "stalks."

- Butterflies have hairs on their wings that detect changes in air pressure.

- You have more pain nerve endings than any other type.

- The least sensitive part of your body is the middle of your back.

- Shivering is the way your body tries to stay warm.

- An earache is caused by too much fluid putting pressure on your eardrum. Earaches are often the result of an infection, allergies, or a virus.

Senses quiz

The answers to these questions can all be found by looking back through the book. See how many you get right. You can check your answers on page 56.

1) How many main senses do we have?
   A—three
   B—four
   C—five

2) What controls our senses?
   A—brain
   B—muscles
   C—heart

3) What is the black circle in the center of the eye called?
   A—pupil
   B—iris
   C—retina

4) A dragonfly's eye is made up of . . .
   A—4,000 parts
   B—30,000 parts
   C—1,000 parts

5) Why might you feel sick on a boat?
   A—your brain gets confused
   B—your eyes get confused
   C—your legs get confused

6) Crickets have ears on their . . .
   A—tongue
   B—back
   C—front legs

7) When do bats hunt?
   A—at night
   B—in the morning
   C—just after lunchtime

8) What does a female moth do when she is ready to mate?
   A—makes a high-pitched noise
   B—gives off a special scent
   C—dances

9) How many main flavors are there?
   A—three
   B—four
   C—five

10) Butterflies have tongues, but what do they also use to taste?
   A—nose
   B—wings
   C—feet

11) What is the most sensitive part of an elephant's body?
   A—ears
   B—trunk
   C—tail

12) What happens to the hairs on your skin when you are scared?
   A—they grow more quickly
   B—they lie flat
   C—they stand on end

Find out more 55

Books to read

Body Science: The Senses by Rufus Bellamy,
    Franklin Watts, 2004

*I Wonder Why Lemons Taste Sour: And
    Other Questions about Senses* by
    Deborah Chancellor, Kingfisher, 2007

The Kingfisher Book of the Human Body
    by Dr. Patricia Macnair, Kingfisher,
    2005

My Amazing Body: Senses by Angela
    Royston, Heinemann, 2004

Understanding the Human Body: Senses by
    Carol Ballard, Rosen Central, 2010

*What Happens When You Use Your
    Senses?* by Jacqui Bailey, PowerKids
    Press, 2008

Places to visit

Science Museum of Minnesota,
Saint Paul, Minnesota
www.smm.org/visit/humanbody/
Visit the Human Body Gallery, featuring
interactive displays and exhibits exploring
what makes us human and what keeps
us alive.

Maryland Science Center, Baltimore,
Maryland
www.mdsci.org/exhibits/your-body.html
Learn about what happens inside your
body every day. *Your Body: The Inside
Story* explores the sounds, smells, sights,
and sensations of human life, including a
walk-in "beating heart chamber" and a
"symphony" of body digestion noises.

Websites

*www.bbc.co.uk/science/humanbody/
body/*
Click on the "Nervous system" section.
This contains information, animations,
and quizzes about human senses.

*http://dsc.discovery.com/tv/human-
body/explorer/explorer.html*
An interactive website with activities such
as putting the correct pieces together to
build your own three-dimensional eye!

*http://faculty.washington.edu/chudler/
introb.html*
An interesting website with information,
activities, games, and quizzes about the
nervous system and senses.

Senses quiz answers

1) C	7) A
2) A	8) B
3) A	9) B
4) B	10) C
5) A	11) B
6) C	12) C